TWELVE
EASY SCARLATTI SONATAS

STUDY EDITION

selected and edited by

ALFRED MIROVITCH

Today, almost 200 years after the death of Domenico Scarlatti (1757), hundreds of his sonatas are still practically unknown to musicians, students and the public. This seems amazing at a time when there exists an almost unprecedented interest in harpsichord music, and when Scarlatti sonatas are listed on the program of scores of piano recitals.

And yet, this fact becomes easily understandable if one is acquainted with the history of publication of Scarlatti's compositions.

Only a small fraction of his enormous output was published during the lifetime of the composer: (1) the thirty sonatas known as the "Original Edition," with a dedication by the composer (date and place of publication uncertain); (2) two small collections published by Thomas Roseingrave, a friend of Scarlatti, about 1735, and 12 sonatas published by John W'organ (1752), both in London.

About a hundred years later, in 1839, Haslinger in Vienna published Carl Czerny's edition of 200 sonatas, and in 1864 Farrenc in Paris included 130 sonatas in his "Tresor des Pianistes."

Then, during the second half of the 19th century, Hans von Bülow, Carl Tausig, Emil Sauer, Buonamici, and others, edited and "transcribed" a number of the sonatas in conformity with the prevailing "romantic" trend and the florid pianistic style of the 19th century, frequently "correcting" and often mutilating the original texts. For many years, and until comparatively recent times, Scarlatti works were played and known almost exclusively in the form of these few transcriptions and "corrected" editions.

It was only at the beginning of this century—about 150 years after Scarlatti's death—that Alessandro Longo completed the first and only comprehensive and authoritative edition of all known 545 Scarlatti works, using available manuscript copies and retaining the original texts.

Scarlatti entitled the Original Edition of 30 sonatas: "Exercizi per gravicembalo" (Exercises for harpsichord"). This title has a special meaning applicable to all Scarlatti sonatas: in each he poses to the player a particular and very definite problem of technique or rhythm, dexterity, speed, sonority or tone color.

In this sense we may perhaps say that the history of "Etudes" in piano literature has its beginnings in the Scarlatti Sonatas.

Scarlatti was perhaps the first composer who wrote "out" of the keyboard and for the keyboard. It is real pianist's music: everything sounds well and "lies" well for the fingers.

Burney, in his "Journeys" quotes Scarlatti answering a friend who commented upon the considerable difficulties of the sonatas : "Nature gave me ten fingers, and my instrument can keep them all occupied—I see no reason why I shouldn't use them all."

In compiling the present small collection, the editor used the text of the Longo edition for nine of the sonatas; the John W'organ book of 1752 was used for Nos. 9 and 10 of this volume, and the text for No. 12 was taken from the "Tresor des Pianistes."

The original texts as found in these sources have been given unaltered. All marks of interpretation, however, including dynamics, phrasing, slurring, shading, pedaling, as well as fingering and interpretation of embellishments, are by the present editor.

The editor's annotations at the head of each sonata are intended to focus the attention of the player on the particular musical or technical problem inherent in each piece, and to offer suggestions for purposeful and concentrated study.

In conclusion, the editor wishes to emphasize that the present collection has been compiled and edited to serve as a "study" edition, and as an introduction to the style and technique of Scarlatti—a preparation for the more difficult and elaborate works of the composer. All of the 12 sonatas in this edition are comparatively easy (of about fourth to fifth grade difficulty), yet they all are characteristically "Scarlatti", fully expressive of the vitality, charm and refined wit of the composer's style.

A. M.

2

1
(Longo 423)

This Sonata-Aria should be played with all the plain, unadorned simplicity and gentle lyricism that its content implies. The *r.h.* should "sing" throughout, but with a limpid, rather small tone, and not exuberantly, in the "romantic" manner. To further emphasize the classical restraint inherent in the music, the editor suggests that no pedal be used. The *l.h.* part, so often carelessly treated in similar compositions, should fully support the "song" of the *r.h.* in every shading and tone quality.

Molto moderato (♪=100)

2
(Longo 83)

The task here is to produce an evenly flowing legato: Play each of the long four-bar phrases as if singing them in one breath. A supple wrist with lateral movements, and fingers that always remain close to the keys "gliding" from one position to the next, will help greatly to achieve this. The massive sound effect of the *l.h.* chords in the last four bars will be enhanced if these chords are played sonorously but not too loudly. The pedal, as suggested by the editor, should be strictly half-pedal, not full.

4

3

(Longo 79)

Here, as in the preceding Sonata, a smooth, even legato finger work is a basic requirement. Do not neglect the simple *l.h.* part: the single bass notes must always be played with enough tone volume to clearly show the harmonic structure. Use pedal for the charming "horn call" and "echo" effects only, as indicated.

Allegro commodo (♩:112-120)

4
(Longo 84)

Throughout this Sonata there must never be either a break or the slightest hesitancy in the time beat. The rhythm should be clearly punctuated by brisk phrase or group accents. Staccatos must be dry, short and sharp and should always be played with the firm, "steely" fingertips that are a primary condition of any real staccato. All finger work should be well articulated: connected non legato.

Allegro con brio (♩ = 100)

5
(Longo 97)

To achieve the swaying, gentle yet steady dance rhythm of this Minuet, the first beat of each bar should be definitely stressed. However, rather than a straight accent, a gently increased pressure of the finger, through a supple wrist motion, will produce just that slightly deeper tone quality which will emphasize and not accentuate the beat. Strict time should be kept, no "accelerandi" or "ritenuti." The editor prefers not to use any pedal.

Tempo di Minuetto (♩ = 108-116)

6

(Longo 58)

Here we have the Scarlatti of steely rhythm, boundless vitality and almost ruthless energy and vigor, yet of an entrancing sonority and tone color, novel in his own day and certainly no less effective or "pianistic" in our time. The *l.h.* part should be practiced carefully and consistently: the chords must sound "full"—all notes of even strength—but never heavy, and the eighth-note chords should be lighter than the quarter-note chords which occur on the first beat of the measure. The mordents should be executed with great precision, exactly on the beat.

7
(Longo 93)

Scarlatti, who spent many years of his adult life in Spain, seems to have been keenly interested in and profoundly affected by the Spanish folk music idiom. A distinctly Spanish flavor apparent in many of his sonatas is also evident in this work: a Spanish "song" in sonata form. The prevailing tone color should therefore be a quasi-legato with due regard for phrasing (as indicated by slurs). The frequently recurring sigh-like motive should be made especially expressive by withdrawing the hand swiftly and softly after playing each group. The repeated notes (as in bar 6) should *not* be staccato, but should be played *within* the key—that is, with the fingers remaining in constant touch with the key surface.

Allegretto giocoso (♩ = 92-100)

sempre senza Ped.

8
(Longo 94)

This short but extremely brilliant Sonata is full to the brim with vitality, energy and joyfulness, and it is the task of the performer to give full and intense expression to these qualities, to make the work live and throb! First comes mechanical perfection, with precise and brisk finger articulation; secondly, machine-like exactitude in time, and thirdly, energetic and clear phrase accents as suggested by the editor. Notice the sudden changes from *f* to *p* and vice versa. No pedal is to be used.

Allegro (♩ : 104-112)

senza Ped.

9

(Longo 388)

A priceless study for evenness in broken chord technique (especially for the *l.h.*) and for the cultivation of that light, short yet firm staccato so characteristic of the Scarlatti "Style." Pay special attention to the staccati in the *l.h.*, and be sure to have the two hands play with absolutely equal clarity and tone quality throughout the entire piece.

Un poco presto ($\bullet$ $\cdot$ $= 60$-72)

senza Ped.

10
(*Longo 358*)

To achieve a brilliant, yet graceful and smooth performance, concentrated attention must be devoted to two points: (1) The swift crossing of the *r.h.* over the *l.h.* should be executed close to the keys (——) not (——) and with firm and pointed fingertips. The "ostinato" triplet figure in the *l.h.* should be played with perfect evenness and without accents. The pedal, as suggested by the editor, will slightly prolong each low bass note, thereby gently increasing sonority.

11
(Longo 413)

This famous Sonata, known to every pianist as "Pastorale," and played by many thousands in the Tausig transcription in E minor, is given here in its original form, without any added notes. The simplicity, straightforwardness and naiveté of this original version is infinitely more appealing to the editor than the rich sonorities with which Tausig chose to "embellish" the piece. A quasi-legato and a limpid, flowing cantabile are absolutely necessary, but avoid an overly sonorous tone quality. The pedal may be used, as indicated, but it should at all times be half-pedal, not full. Staccatos, rather than being too short, should be played as lightly detached notes.

Allegro non troppo (♩·= 66)

12

(Longo 386)

Mechanical perfection in finger action and faultless precision in time and rhythm are the two basic requirements here. The finger action should be a *connected* non legato: each finger must strike the key—not depress or fall on it—to achieve the martellato-like precision and tone quality required. The editor suggests the frequent and consistent use of the metronome for the study of this as well as similar pieces: an eighth note to the beat for slower study, and later a quarter note to the beat.

Allegro non troppo (♩ : 104-112)